THE PRINTER'S MANUAL
AN ILLUSTRATED HISTORY

The Printer's Manual

AN ILLUSTRATED HISTORY

*Classic and Unusual Texts on Printing
from the Seventeenth, Eighteenth,
and Nineteenth Centuries*

David Pankow

RIT CARY GRAPHIC ARTS PRESS
ROCHESTER, NEW YORK
2005

The Printer's Manual – An Illustrated History
by David Pankow

Published and distributed by
RIT Cary Graphic Arts Press
90 Lomb Memorial Drive
Rochester, New York 14623-5604
http://wally.rit.edu/cary/carypress.html

Printed in the United States
ISBN 0-9759651-0-7

Cover image: Taylor's Double Cylinder printing press,
from Thomas F. Adams, *Typographia: or the Printer's
Instructor; A Brief Sketch of the Origin, Rise and Progress
of the Typographic Art.*

CONTENTS

Introduction

AS PRINTING FROM MOVABLE TYPE was perfected in the fifteenth century, the mysteries of its practice were guarded by a privileged few. Gutenberg himself took great pains to avoid disclosing the techniques he had developed for the rapid multiplication of books, only to see the fruits of his long research snatched away from him by his chief creditor, Johann Fust, in an ignominious lawsuit. To make matters worse, tradition has it that Gutenberg's apprentice Peter Schöffer took the secrets of the new craft, joined forces with Fust, and, together with his new partner, reaped the benefits of his former master's toil.

The rapid spread of the new art, however, depended on the development of a reliable mechanism for transferring knowledge, and printers naturally adapted the established practices of the medieval craft guilds. The essential facts and techniques were passed on from master printer to journeyman to apprentice, together with all of the attendant ceremonies of initiation and pledges of fellowship. Like a dynastic succession, the management of an early printing office was often kept within a particular family, sometimes for generations. In this way, the art of printing was preserved and sustained, often carefully veiled from outsiders, and always the product of years of close study and practice.

By the end of the seventeenth century, however, the pioneers of manufacturing technology and scientific inquiry were prying away at the rotting doors of medieval trade secrecy. One of this new breed, a sometime printer by the name of Joseph Moxon, found a congenial climate in which to publish his *Mechanick Exercises*. The work was issued in 1683 and contained, among other treatises, the first printer's manual in any language. Moxon had mastered a number of mathematical and mechanical skills; his justification for sharing them with the "good and curious workman" appeared in the preface to volume one:

> The Lord Bacon in his 'Natural History' reckons that philosophy would be improved by having the secrets of all trades lye open; not only because much experimental philosophy is caught among them, but also that the trades themselves might by a philosopher be improved. Besides, I find that one trade may borrow many eminent helps in work of another trade.

Though successors to Moxon followed slowly at first (only two more English manuals of any significance were published between 1683 and 1800), the nineteenth century saw a proliferation of printing and a sizeable increase in the number of manuals, dictionaries, tracts, and other works written about it. Nearly every one of them owes something to Moxon, either for material borrowed (sometimes generously) or the inspiration for existing at all. Many of the customs of a printing office were first described by Moxon. Some, like the printers' Wayzgoose, survive as the quaint recreations of historians or amateur printing societies. Others still endure today, but in a strange, transmuted fashion. The Chappel, for example, the customary term, "time out of mind" says Moxon, for a printing-house, lived well on into the twentieth century in the production departments of newspapers. There, a chappel denoted the room in which the employees sat before being called to their stations by their union shop steward!

This selection shows the history of printing manuals, from 1683 to the end of the nineteenth century, including some of the rarest in existence. The focus has largely been on English and American works, though manuals have been published in many languages. A few early French and German manuals have been admitted because of their connection to Moxon, or because of their intrinsic interest to the development of the genre. Some titles, like *The History of Printing,* published by the Society for Promoting Christian Knowledge, are included for their thorough accounts of printing-office practice and their instructive value, even though, strictly speaking, they are not printer's manuals. As for why a catalog of this sort should compel the attention of aspiring printers, graphic arts students, and historians, one need go no further then to Lawrence Wroth's essay "Corpus Typographicum," published in *Typographic Heritage* (New York: The Typophiles, 1949). He writes:

> The thoughtful printer of today still goes to those manuals to learn the ancient traditions of type, composition, and impression, for despite the improvements worked by the centuries in mechanical means, the fundamental materials, instruments, and operations of typography have remained unchanged … It is not as relics of a misty past, therefore, that I propose to write of them here, but as living, ageless books of instruction with lessons for all of us who are concerned with the practice, theory, and history of the printing craft.

David Pankow

THE PRINTER'S MANUAL
AN ILLUSTRATED HISTORY

Joseph Moxon

Mechanick Exercises: Or, the Doctrine of Handy-Works, Applied to the Art of Printing. London: Printed for Joseph Moxon, 1683.

THE SON OF A PRINTER, Joseph Moxon learned the trade of printing early, but also achieved expertise in other disciplines, including mathematics, astronomy, globe- and map-making, and wood-working. His greatest contemporary recognition came when he was appointed to the post of Hydrographer to the King, a position in which he was responsible for maintaining official charts of ocean navigation routes.

Moxon's most enduring achievement and the source of his lasting fame was the *Mechanick Exercises*, a series of useful tracts on "handy-works" published in two volumes. The second of these was devoted entirely to the arts of printing and typefounding. Herbert Davis and Harry Carter, in their exhaustively annotated 1962 edition of the *Exercises*, note that Moxon's book "was by forty years the earliest manual of printing in any language, and it put in writing a knowledge that was wholly traditional. Though he did not himself live in a great age of printing, he described with great care the tools and the skilled movements that had produced the masterpieces of the craft in better days."

No manual ever provided more information about the construction and proper management of the printer's primary tool in those days, the wooden common press; a modern-day reader, caught long enough under the manual's spell, could still follow the directions and copper-plate diagrams and build such a press today. "A typographer ought to be a man of science," said Moxon in justification of his elaborately detailed manual, and he goes on to raise that individual to an even nobler elevation: "By a typographer I do not mean a *printer*, as he is vulgarly accounted … But by a typographer I mean such a one who, by his own judgement, from solid reasoning with himself, can either perform or direct others to perform, from the beginning to the end all the hand-works and physical operations relating to typographie. Such a scientific man was doubtless he who was the first inventor of typographie."

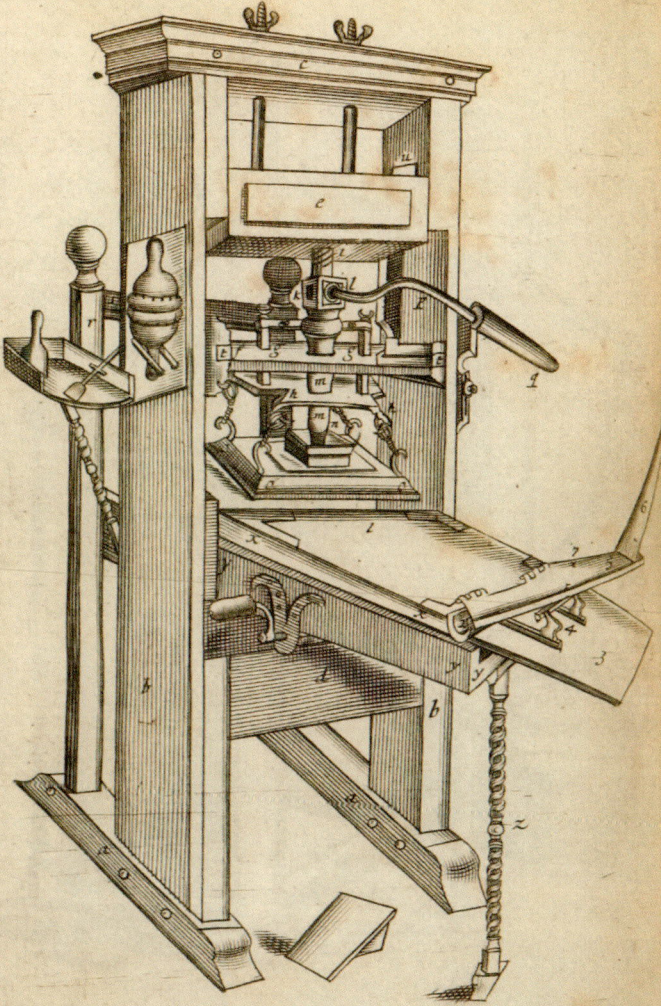

Plate 4.

3

Joseph Moxon

Moxon's Mechanick Exercises . . . A Literal Reprint in Two Volumes of the First Edition Published in the Year 1683. New-York: The Typothetae of the City of New-York, 1896.

THEODORE LOW DE VINNE CONTRIBUTED the preface and notes to this beautiful edition of Moxon, served on the committee which commissioned its publication, and supervised its printing at the De Vinne Press. Only 450 copies were issued. It is a fairly close type facsimile of the original, and, as De Vinne tells us in the Preface, "this edition … is a line-for-line and page-for-page reprint of the original text … The type selected for this work was cast from matrices struck with the punches (made about 1740) of the first Caslon. It is of the same large English body as that of the original, but a trifle smaller as to face, and not as compressed as the type used by Moxon; but it repeats many of his peculiarities, and fairly reproduces the more important mannerisms of the printing of the seventeenth century."

MOXON'S
MECHANICK EXERCISES

OR THE DOCTRINE OF HANDY-WORKS
APPLIED TO THE ART OF

PRINTING

A LITERAL REPRINT IN TWO VOLUMES OF
THE FIRST EDITION PUBLISHED IN THE YEAR 1683

WITH PREFACE AND NOTES BY
THEO. L. DE VINNE

VOLUME I

NEW-YORK
THE TYPOTHETÆ OF THE CITY OF NEW-YORK
MDCCCLXXXXVI

James Watson

The History of the Art of Printing, Containing an Account of its Invention and Progress in Europe ...Edinburgh: James Watson, 1713.

> Great Blest Master-Printer, Come
>> Into Thy composing-Room:
> Wipe away our foul Offences;
>> Make, O make our souls and senses,
> The Upper and the Lower Cases;
>> And Thy large alphabet of Graces
> The Letter, which being ever fit,
>> O haste thou to Distribute it:
> For there is (I make Account)
>> No imperfection in the Fount.

THUS BEGINS a wonderful extended poetic metaphor on the relationship between God the master printer and the creatures of his creation, symbolized as pages of type. The poem appears at the end of James Watson's *Art of Printing* which, aside from containing so striking a meditation, stands as a valuable document between Moxon's manual of 1683 and Smith's of 1755. Though Watson is not a printer's manual per se (it is more a brief history of the art), it does contain some interesting information on early eighteenth century printing practices in Scotland. There is also a specimen of the types used in Watson's printing office and a folding illustration of ornaments and factotum initials. Very few copies of the original exist, so that most libraries must content themselves with a facsimile made from the St. Bride's Institute library copy, published in 1965 by the Gregg Press, Ltd., of London. The copy on view here was once in the renowned library of the American Type Founders Company.

FUndamental Alterations bring inevitable Perils. If the Paper chance to have a Blot; remember, the Blot is no Part of the Copy. A full **T**ongue, and an empty Brain, are seldom parted.

T*Ake heed of that Honour which thy Wealth hath purchased thee; for it is neither lasting, nor thine own. That which is bought with Gold, will hardly be maintain'd with Steel.*

7

J. H. G. Ernesti

Die Wol-eingerichtete Büchdrückerey, mit hundert und achtzehen Teutsch, Lateinisch, Griechisch und Hebraischen Schrifften … Nürnberg, Johann Andred Endters, 1721.

DISTINGUISHED BY ITS OBLONG FORMAT and its famous frontispiece engraving of a printing office, this rare manual contains an account of famous early printers followed by engraved portraits and biographies of the prominent printers of Nuremberg. The work continues with showings of type and music specimens, ornaments, and a variety of tables and imposition schemes that betray its bias towards language and composition rather than the technical details of presswork. Many of the pages are printed in two colors. It concludes with Johann Rist's popular dramatic poem on printing, *Depositio Cornuti Typographici.*

9

Martin Dominique Fertel

La Science pratique de l'Imprimerie conteneant des instructions tres-faciles pour se perfectionner dans cet art. Saint Omer: Marchand Libraire, 1723.

FERTEL'S *La Science pratique* WAS PUBLISHED forty years after Moxon and is acknowledged by scholars to have been as important to French printers as its more famous predecessor was to English printers. An exhaustive comparison of the two books has shown that Fertel made an important and original contribution to the understanding and practice of printing. Whether he knew of Moxon is not known; Lawrence Wroth, however, points out a statement in the preface in which the author notes that he had failed "throughout many years of search to find in print any book of practical utility to the typographic workman."

Fertel includes good sections on book design and the history and use of accents and diacritical marks. His is a scholarly work with a strong emphasis on making books of quality, from the choice of typefaces to the selection of appropriate format. Later manuals like that of Smith (1755) depended almost as much on Fertel for material as they did on Moxon, hence its inclusion in this catalog.

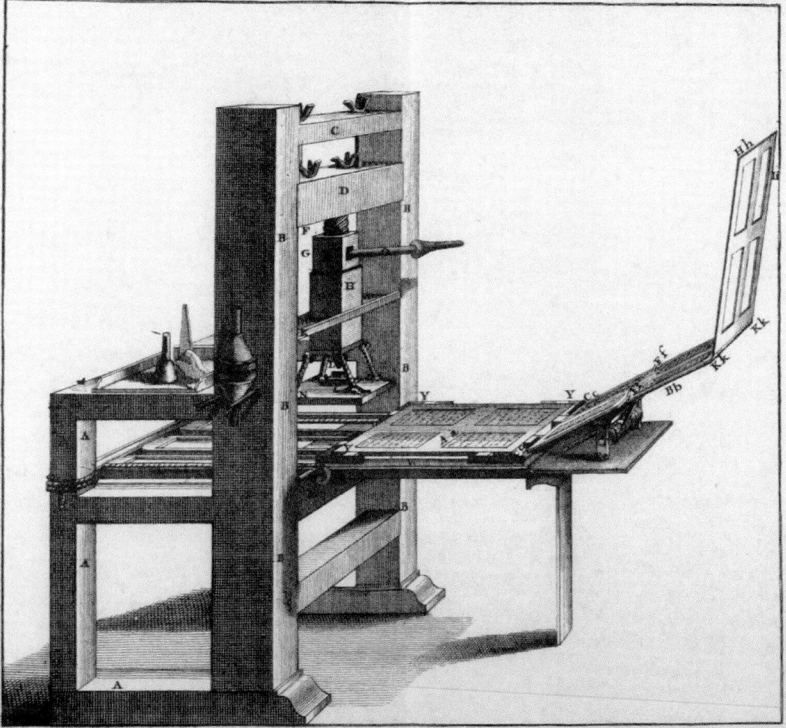

II

Christian Friedrich Gessner

Die so nöthig als nützliche Buchdruckerkunst und Schriftgiesserey, mit ihren Schriften, Formaten und allen dazu gehörigen Instrumenten abgebildet . . . 2 of 4 volumes. Leipzig: Christian Friedrich Gessner, 1740.

A CCORDING TO D. B. UPDIKE "this work was to an eighteenth-century printer and amateur, what Fournier's *Manuel Typographique* was at that date to Frenchmen of similar tastes." There is a good deal of information on the invention of printing, as well as accounts and portraits of German printers, especially those of Leipzig. The production of this manual must have entailed many nightmarish hours in the bindery, since it is laden with copperplate engravings, folding plates and various tip-ins illustrating printers' marks, orthographical tables of exotic alphabets, case layouts, and all the technical equipment that one would expect to find in a printing office and type foundry of the period. The handsome frontispiece engraving of an eighteenth-century printing office was adapted from Ernesti's 1721 manual. Updike, however, found it most useful for its inclusion of the 1739 *Schrift-Probe*, or specimen of types, of Bernhard Christoph Breitkopf, the most important German founder of the eighteenth century. A curious addition at the end of volume 2 is a treatise on printing by Martin Luther, whose canny use of the new process in the sixteenth century was largely responsible for the spread of the Reformation.

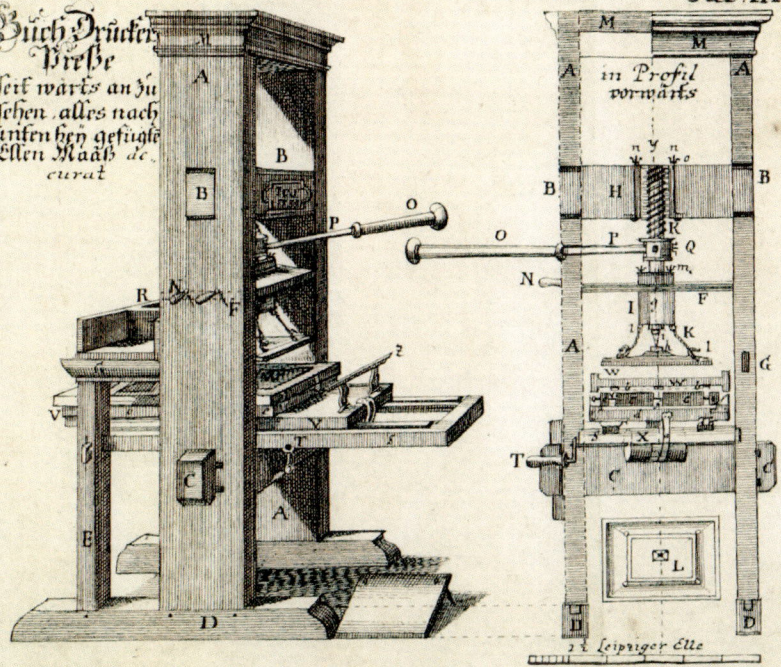

Tab. III

Buch Drucker
Presse
seit wärts an zu
sehen alles nach
untren hey gefügte
Ellen Maaß de
curat

in Profil
vorwärts

R. del.

D.V.B. sc.

3 ½ Leipziger Elle

Pierre Simon Fournier, le jeune

Manuel typographique, utile aux gens de lettres, & a ceux qui exercent les différentes parties de l'art de l'imprimerie. Paris: Imprimé par l'auteur …, 1764–66.

"TYPOGRAPHY," said Fournier, "may be regarded as consisting of three parts, each distinct and indispensable, namely, punchcutting, founding, and printing. The practice of the different branches produces artists of three different kinds, the first punch cutters, the second founders, and the third printers, but only he who combines a knowledge of all three branches is fit to be styled a Typographer."

With that view in mind, Pierre Simon Fournier (1712–1768) set out to write a manual of typography, to be published in four volumes. He certainly possessed the requisite qualifications. Though a little shaky on the history of printing—he did not know, for example, of Moxon's work—Fournier had mastered a complex array of typefounding and printing technologies.

His scheme called for the first volume to contain an account of punchcutting and founding, the second to be devoted to printing, the third to contain a treatise on typographers, and the fourth to be a collection of type specimens. In the end, only the first and the fourth were published, since the two middle volumes had not been completed before Fournier's death in 1768. Had the entire series been published as planned, it would have rivaled Moxon for breadth of coverage. As it was, most writers after Moxon tended to concentrate on composition and presswork. Though incomplete, Fournier's work is one of the monuments of printing history, not only for its thorough account of typefounding techniques and practices, but because it introduced the concept of the point-system to the typographic community. While his specific dimensions for the point (and the body-sizes of types based on it) were later superseded by those of the Didot system, no one would argue that credit for this momentous reform belongs to Fournier.

TABLE GÉNÉRALE
DE LA PROPORTION
des différens Corps de Caractères.

ÉCHELLE FIXE
de 144 points Typographiques.

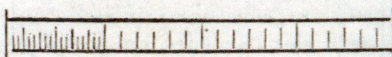

Nomb.	CORPS.	Points
1	PARISIENNE.	5
2	NOMPAREILLE.	6
3	MIGNONE.	7
4	PETIT-TEXTE.	8
5	GAILLARDE.	9
6	PETIT-ROMAIN. — 2 Parisiennes.	10
7	PHILOSOPHIE. = 1 Parif. 1 Nom-pareille.	11
8	CICÉRO. — 2 Nomp. = 1 Pari-sienne, 1 Mignone.	12
9	SAINT-AUGUSTIN. — 2 Mignones. = 1 Nompareille, 1 Petit-texte.	14

Philip Luckombe

The History and Art of Printing ... London: Printed by W. Adlard and J. Browne, 1771.

Though Moxon had been published almost a hundred years earlier, only the manuals of Fertel and John Smith (1755) had been issued between it and that of Luckombe. Aware of the shortage of good instructional material on printing, the author notes in his introduction that:

> Books on this important subject are become extremely scarce, owing to their being deposited in the libraries of the curious, which make them but seldom seen in the common catalogues of Booksellers, and when they are, their price is too high for the generality of readers.

While the woodcut illustrations are somewhat crudely rendered and the text is largely derivative, Luckombe's manual quickly became popular. Described by Lawrence Wroth as a "literary hack," Luckombe was not overly fastidious about acknowledging his sources. In fact, Wroth states that the historical portion is "a treacherous source for the historian. In taking over sections from Moxon and Smith, ... the compiler either did not bother to eliminate from the texts of his predecessors matter that was no longer applicable to the conditions of his own time, or else he allowed such matter to remain through ignorance of its implications." In fact, Luckombe borrows a portrait from Moxon and identifies it as that of Gutenberg when, in fact, it is actually Moxon's portrait of Jan Laurens Coster, the Dutch candidate for inventor of printing.

One of the book's interesting features is the liberal and inventive use of ornaments throughout; they are used as borders, as frames for initials, and as head and tailpiece arrangements. A particularly important feature is the inclusion of "A Specimen of Printing Types" by William Caslon.

THE PRINTING PRESS.

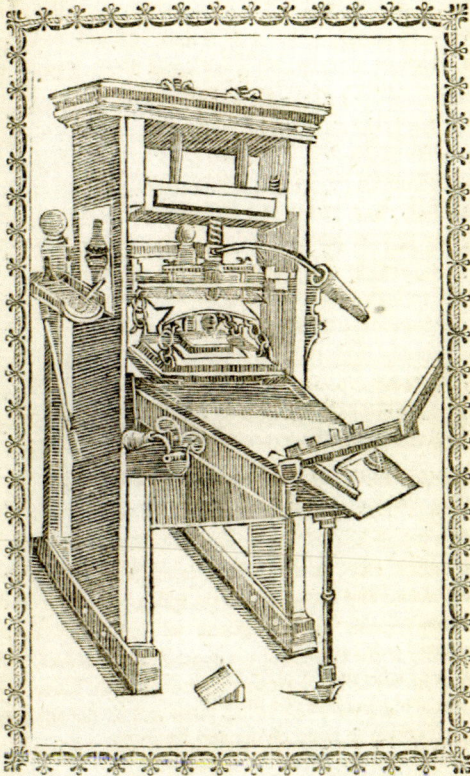

This Machine confifts of the following parts,
The Feet, Cheeks, Cap, Winter, Head, Till, Hofe, Garter, Hooks, Spindle, Worm, Nut, Eye of the Spindle, Shank of the Spindle, Toe of the Spindle, Plattin, Bar, Handle of the Bar, Hind Pofts, Hind Rails, Wedges of the Till, Carriage, Outer Frame of the Carriage, Iron Ribs, Wooden

John Smith

The Printer's Grammar, Containing a Concise History of the Origin of Printing; Also an Examination of the … Different Sizes of Types Cast by Letter Founders … Chiefly from Smith's Edition. London: Printed by L. Wayland, 1787.

Typical of late eighteenth century practice, the number of words on the title page of this manual continues well beyond what is recorded above, leaving no doubt as to exactly what is to be covered within its pages. This is a curious book because it has been awkwardly cobbled together from earlier sources; it is clearly derivative of Moxon and Fertel by way of Smith and Luckombe. Indeed, most of the technical information is identical to that contained in Luckombe's manual, who in turn had assembled it from Smith. Davis and Carter, in their annotated version of Moxon's *Mechanick Exercises*, write, "the book has the air of a hastily improvised vehicle for the type specimen … by Edmund Fry & Co."—just as Luckombe's manual had contained a Caslon specimen. The Fry material is quite beautiful, and includes the celebrated printer's flowers and ornaments for which the foundry was famous.

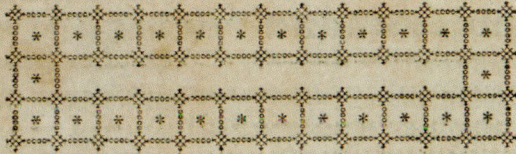

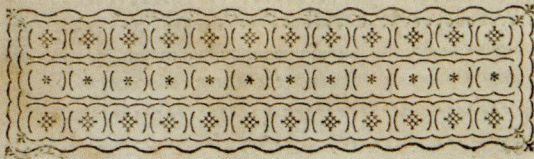

19

Caleb Stower

The Printer's Grammar; or Introduction to the Art of Print-ing. Containing a Concise History of the Art with the Improve-ments in the Practice of Printing, for the Last Fifty Years. London: Printed by the editor for B. Crosby and Co., 1808.

S TOWER IMMEDIATELY ANNOUNCES the timeliness of his manual by including a frontispiece illustration of the Stanhope Press, a rela-tively recent invention. In fact, he dedicates his book to Earl Stanhope, its inventor, saying, "your indefatigable persevering genius has investi-gated almost every article of human ingenuity which is connected with the welfare and happiness of man."

The historical section is new, while the material on composition and correction are derived from Smith. The section on the construction of presses is new, but the chapter "Practical Directions to Pressmen" is mostly taken from the seventeenth-century manual of Moxon. But as Lawrence Wroth notes, "the work is Moxon filtered through Smith and Luckombe with such intelligent rephrasing, omission, and addition as show that the matter itself had passed through Stower's mind as well as through his hands before it was committed to paper." Compared to the skewed illustrations in Luckombe with their odd perspective, those in Stower are quite accurately drawn. Chapter 10 contains an interesting array of exotic alphabets adapted from the *Pantographia* of Dr. Edmund Fry.

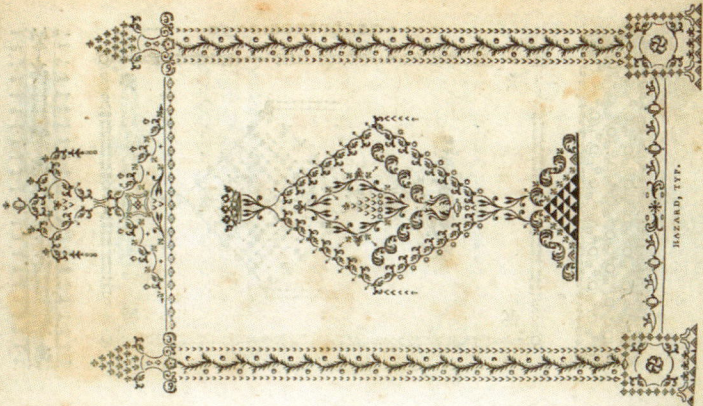

HAZARD, TYP.

Caleb Stower

The Printer's Manual, An Abridgment of Stower's Grammar, Comprising all the Plans in that Work for Imposing Forms, Several Tables and Other Useful Articles. Boston: Printed and published by R. & C. Crocker, 1817.

UNTIL 1978, THE EARLIEST American printer's manual was thought to be the 1818 *Printer's Guide* of C. S. Van Winkle. Alexander Lawson of the School of Printing at RIT, however, discovered the existence of this manual, published in 1817, a year before Van Winkle. The Crocker edition is slim and contains only those passages from Stower's manual of 1808 that pertain to the responsibilities of compositors, proofreaders and pressmen. In fact, there is nothing original to the work. Despite its shabby appearance and borrowed text, it does occupy a place of preeminence in American printing history.

The copy shown here is tattered and stained, but lives in a very handsome original nineteenth century binding. Only three copies are known: one at Yale, one at the Graphic Arts Technical Foundation Library in Sewickley, PA, and the Cary copy.

THE

PRINTER'S MANUAL,

AN

ABRIDGMENT

OF

STOWER'S GRAMMAR;

COMPRISING ALL THE PLANS IN THAT WORK FOR IMPOSING
FORMS, SEVERAL TABLES AND OTHER USEFUL ARTICLES.

With a Copperplate Engraving,
Being an Exemplification of Typographical Marks.

BOSTON:
PRINTED AND PUBLISHED BY R. & C. CROCKER,
No. 3, SUFFOLK BUILDINGS.
1817.

C. S. Van Winkle

The Printers' Guide; or, an Introduction to the Art of Printing; Including an Essay on Punctuation ... New-York: Printed and published by C. S. Van Winkle, 1818.

Though Van Winkle's *Guide* can technically no longer be considered the first American manual—the recent discovery of a much abridged version of Stower's manual published a year earlier in Boston preempts it of that distinction—Van Winkle's work was much more substantial and widely circulated, reaching several editions.

Van Winkle is admirably candid in his introduction, pointing out that his work owed much to the manual of Caleb Stower. "We have," he writes, "selected from Mr. Stower's Grammar all that was considered of practical utility to the printer." There is no introductory history of printing, readers being referred to the work published eight years earlier by Isaiah Thomas, the Worcester printer and historian of American printing.

Though certain prescriptive dicta of Moxon still survive, the new iron printing machinery then coming into use required its own set of descriptive matter and instructions on use. Thus, for example, there are notes on the new iron handpresses and an account of the Columbian press, though George Clymer, its Philadelphia inventor, had already left American shores for greener pastures in England. The book concludes with fine specimens of the printing types from the E. White and the D. and G. Bruce Foundries.

By 1836, three editions had been published. A twelve-page history of printing was added, but the type specimens were eliminated. Two facsimile editions have been published. The first was issued in 1970 by the Lakeside Press and is itself an uncommon book, while the second was issued in by Garland Publishing in 1981.

REMEMBER, that *time* is money. He that can earn ten shillings a ~~week~~ by his labour, and goes abroad, sitsidle one half of the day, tho ugh he spend but sixpence during hijs diversion or ~~or~~ idleness, ought not to reckon *that* the only expence: he has really spent, rather or thrown away, five shillings beside. [Remember; that money is *credit*. If a man lets his money lie in my hands after it is due.

He gives me the interest, or so much as I can make of it, a considerable sum where a mna has good ~~and large~~ credit, and makes good use of it.

Remember, that money is of a prolific, generating nature. Money can beget money, and its offspring can beget more, and so on. Five shillings turned is six, turned again it is seven and three pence, and so on, till it becomes a hundred pounds. The more there is of it, &c.

during that time. This amounts to

William Savage

Practical Hints on Decorative Printing, with Illustrations Engraved on Wood, and Printed in Colours at the Type Press. London: Published for the proprietor by Longman, Hurst, Rees, Orme and Brown, 1822.

WILLIAM SAVAGE ESTABLISHED HIMSELF as a printer in London in 1797 after having spent the early part of his career in Yorkshire. He quickly joined the front rank of printers and became deeply interested in inks for color printing. After some years of experimentation, Savage decided to publish a book on color printing and circulated a prospectus for the printing of 325 copies. Only 227 subscribers actually responded to the prospectus, making *Practical Hints on Decorative Printing* a very rare book today, especially in its large paper format.

Among other innovations, Savage promoted the use of copaiba balsam for the resinous component of ink in order to minimize the common problem of staining. Though few printers ever adopted Savage's formulae, the aromatic balsam made at least one twentieth-century appearance—in the ink used for *The Odyssey* of Homer, printed and published by Bruce Rogers and Emery Walker in 1932.

In addition to a brief history of printing, where Savage comments with admiration on the quality of early printing inks, *Practical Hints* contains discussions on printing presses, fine press-work, and printing types. But the *pièce de résistance* comes with the forty-four full-page wood-engraved illustrations, thirty-three of which are printed in color. One particularly vivid illustration, named "Ode to Mercy," required the use of twenty-nine different blocks. Bigmore and Wyman in their *Bibliography of Printing*, while complimentary overall, described this illustration as "a monstrous abortion—it is horrible—its only merit is in the patience and difficulty with which it was gestated and brought to parturition. I could wish, as Dr. Johnson said of the lady's piece of difficult music, it had been *impossible*."

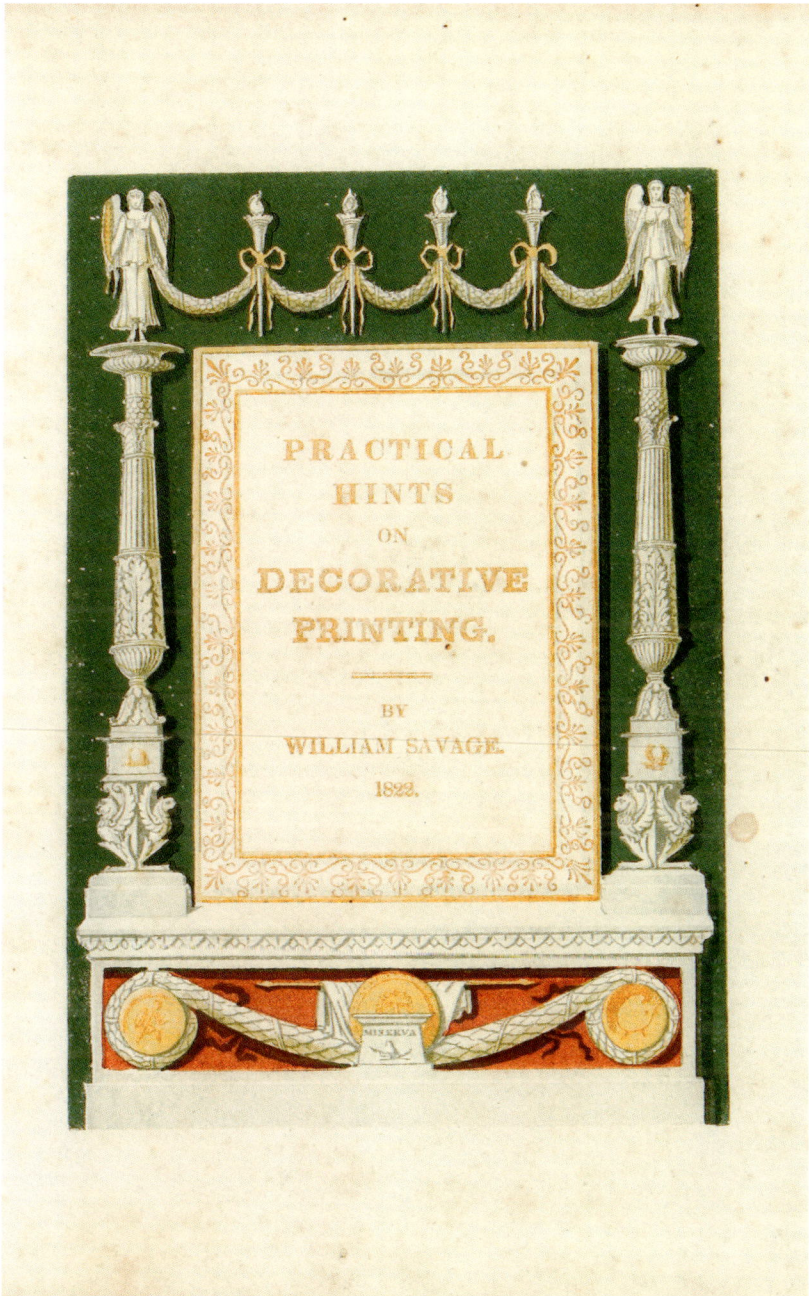

PRACTICAL
HINTS
ON
DECORATIVE
PRINTING.

BY
WILLIAM SAVAGE.
1822.

John Johnson

*Typographia, or the Printers' Instructor: Including an Account of the Origin of Printing...*London: Longman, Hurst, Rees, Orme, Brown & Green, 1824.

THIS EXTRAORDINARY PRINTER'S MANUAL was written and produced by John Johnson, a craftsman known for the quality of his printing. Part of his early career had been spent at one of the earliest of English private presses, the Lee Priory Press of Sir Edgerton Brydges. The books produced there were gems of design and printing and often incorporated wood-engravings of the Thomas Bewick school.

Johnson left Lee Priory in 1817 after a quarrel with his employer and set up as a printer in London where he soon began working on the text of *Typographia*, the book for which he became famous. Its two volumes contain nearly 1,300 pages interspersed with numerous wood-engravings of a very high quality. Some of these engravings were cut by William Harvey, one of the most accomplished pupils of Thomas Bewick.

While much of the historical material in volume one is second-hand, the technical information in the second volume is quite competent and is accompanied by a wealth of anecdote and opinion. Typographically, the work is remarkable for the ornamental borders which frame every page and for the minuteness of the type. There are few printers left today who can comprehend the skills necessary to compose a book of this nature.

550....Typographia.

29

Thomas C. Hansard

Typographia: An Historical Sketch of the Origin and Progress of the Art of Printing; with Practical Directions for Conducting Every Department in an Office. London: Baldwin, Cradock, and Joy, 1825.

IN THE PREFACE, Hansard notes, "this work is partly formed upon the basis of the 'Printer's Grammar' published some years ago by Mr. Stower…The present volume is…intended not only to supply that of Mr. Stower, but to include the choicest portions of every prior publication which has appeared in our language relative to printing."

Hansard's work is generally regarded as one of the most detailed of all nineteenth-century printing manuals, containing splendid, dimensionally accurate wood-engravings of all the technical equipment and miscellaneous devices necessary to run a printing office. All of the important presses of the day are discussed, and Hansard's description of George Clymer's Columbian press is a masterpiece of tongue-in-cheek hyperbole.

In a chapter on fine printing, Hansard condemns many of the modern typefaces, especially those with hair-line serifs. As a practicing printer, Hansard could say with considerable authority that though such types "gave to fine work and early impressions a neatness and finish resembling copper-plate, [thin serifs were] very detrimental, as these sharp edges would not stand for any length of time the action of the press, but either broke off or were blunted, so that the fount soon acquired the appearance of age and long service."

Hansard's *Treatises on Printing and Type-founding* (Edinburgh: 1841), shown here, originally appeared in the seventh edition of the *Encyclopedia Britannica*, but was reprinted as a separate publication in 1841. An important appendix to this work is an essay on lithographic printing written by William Nichol.

PLATE CCCCXIV.

Fac-Simile of the Mentz Psalter, A.D. 1457.

Eatus vir qui non
abiit in ꝯsilio impioꝝ
et in via peccatoꝝu non
stetit: ꞇ in cathedra pesti-
lentie non sedit . Sed
in lege domini volutas

COLOPHONS.

FUST AND SCHŒFFER.

WILLIAM CAXTON.

wynkyn de worde

PAIR CETTAIRE
OYON IOR ET AS MEMOR · DENTE · TENETO · MORI
Pierre Regnault

The Printer. London: Houlston and Stoneman [1833].

THE PURPOSE OF THIS BOOK IS UNCLEAR. It is not a manual in any strict sense, yet it contains practical instructions for case and press. It may have been published to inform parents and young boys about the inside workings of the printing trade, containing just enough detail to intrigue the newcomer. The tone of this small volume is plain without being condescending, and there is no attempt to gloss over the more disagreeable aspects of the printer's life. Acquainted with such a description, the parent of a young boy "having no prospect of maintenance but by the labour of his hands" might decide to place him in a seven-year apprenticeship, leading eventually to a position as a journeyman compositor or pressman.

The author of this treatise liberally sprinkles his narrative with anecdotes and amusing tales of the trade. In a section on slovenly compositors we read of instances "in which an ode to a Grecian *urn* was translated into an ode to a Grecian *nose*; in which Queen Mab was drawn by a team of little *attorneys*, instead of the little *'atomies'* of Shakespeare; and the *aromatic principles* of the English constitution, instead of the *democratic* ..."

To face p. 48.

33

The Penny Magazine of the Society for the Diffusion of Useful Knowledge. No. 107 (London, Oct. 31–Nov. 30, 1833).

DURING THE MONTHS from August to December 1833, *The Penny Magazine,* published in England by Charles Knight, issued a series of four supplements entitled "The Commercial History of a Penny Magazine." The series consisted of essays on papermaking, typefounding, composition, printing, and binding. *The Penny Magazine,* with its liberal use of wood-engraved illustrations, was vastly popular, selling at the phenomenal rate of some 200,000 copies per week. The steady rise in literacy levels during the early nineteenth century was indicative of the great demand for practical knowledge as well as entertainment for its own sake; accounts of manufacturing processes found a ready audience. The supplement shown here describes the processes of composition and stereotyping.

Monthly Supplement of

THE PENNY MAGAZINE

OF THE

Society for the Diffusion of Useful Knowledge.

107.]   October 31, to November 30, 1833.

THE COMMERCIAL HISTORY OF A PENNY MAGAZINE.—No. III.

COMPOSITORS' WORK AND STEREOTYPING.

[Ancient View of a Dutch Printing-Office.]

In a very curious set of prints by L. Galle, after the designs of Stradanus, a painter who flourished in the latter end of the sixteenth century, are represented many operations in the arts, as they were practised at that period. We have copied, as above, his view of a printing-office. On the right is the master printer, a grave, bearded personage, dressed in a fur-trimmed robe, apparently giving some directions to his workmen. These consist of several compositors, comfortably seated on cushioned stools; the dirk of one is in a sheath by his side, and the sword of another rests against a column. This ancient privilege of the compositors of all countries to wear swords still forms a matter of pride with the printers of the present day; for it affords a proof that their art was considered a liberal one, and that men of birth and education were accustomed to practise it. The printers of Paris were thus authorized to wear swords by a royal ordinance of 1571. The costume must have strangely contrasted with the paper cap which the printers of Paris then wore, and which they still wear. Near one of the compositors in our print is an old man in spectacles, who is probably engaged in the business of a reader, which we shall have to explain. The men at work at the two rude presses, the further one inking the types, and the other pulling down the screw which gives the impression, exhibit the mode then employed to work off the sheets, which must have been particularly slow. To this we shall advert when we come to speak of the

Vol. II.

printing press and the machine. Altogether this print appears to show that, in the ancient printing-offices, there were few mechanical aids to labour; and we may infer that the compositors especially, comfortably seated, and somewhat luxuriously clothed, were not much affected by that spirit of restless activity which distinguishes a modern printing-office.

There is a well-authenticated story of an English clergyman, who taught himself the printing art, and carried it on with a persevering devotion to one object, of which we have no other example. This good man had projected a complete body of divinity in a great many volumes. He proposed his scheme to several publishers, but they all rejected it. He then caused copies of several volumes to be printed by subscription. This undertaking failed. He was determined, however, that his literary labours should not be deprived of that chance of immortality which the printing-press, to a certain extent, can bestow. He bought a few types, enough to set up two pages, and thus scantily provided, he undertook the wonderful task of printing, not a small tract, or even one goodly volume, but a great number of volumes. When his two pages were arranged, he printed off fourteen copies at a little press which he had established in his house. The types were then broken up to allow him to print the two next pages; and thus with a tortoise pace he printed away for some twenty years, and at last completed his work in twenty-six volumes,

3 O

Thomas F. Adams

Typographia: or the Printer's Instructor; A Brief Sketch of the Origin, Rise and Progress of the Typographic Art. Philadelphia: Printed and published by the compiler, 1837.

IN COMMENTING ON THE CONNECTION between Adams's *Typographia* and other early American manuals, Lawrence Wroth is "compelled to admit some degree of impatience ... for the practical section ... is the least original of the whole series." Nevertheless, judging by the number of editions it went through, Adams's work was clearly a popular manual. Van Winkle had, at least in the first edition of his manual, acknowledged his debt to Stower's work; Adams, on the other hand, lifted almost his entire text from the *Typographia*s of Johnson and Hansard, but fails to credit either one of them. Wroth fulminated: "it seems to me that by the addition of the following paragraph to his preface of 1864, the compiler added effrontery to the list of his literary sins:"

> Very many of the works heretofore published on this subject, in a practical point of view, have been little else than reprints of old Grammars, chiefly of Smith's, published in London, 1755; although we have in many instances adopted the language of our predecessors, still we have, in general not only compressed the information contained in it, but in all cases made it subservient to our own views and experience.

Though Wroth's barely concealed charge of plagiarism would be regarded today as a very serious offense, the practice of appropriating published material for one's own purposes was all too common in the nineteenth century, since copyright laws were almost non-existent.

However much parts of it might flaunt the laws of literary decency, Adams's manual contains a good introduction to some of the newer mechanical apparatuses being introduced to the printing industry.

THE PHILADELPHIA PRESS.

Charles Henry Timperley

The Printers' Manual; Containing Instructions to Learners, with Scales of Impositions ... together with Practical Directions for Conducting Every Department of a Printing Office. London: H. Johnson, 1838.

TIMPERLEY'S MANUAL IS ONE OF THE SHORTEST of the nineteenth century treatises on printing, concluding its work in a mere 116 pages. After a brief summary of predecessors in the field and a note stating that "it is difficult to fix a starting-post," Timperley does finally commence with a essay on punctuation. Like other printers before him, Timperley mistrusted authors and advised them "to leave the pointing entirely to printers." Such a practice would minimize the chances that the printer's mind would be "confused by commas and semi colons placed indiscriminately, in the hurry of writing, without any regard to propriety."

In 1839 Timperley published his *Encyclopedia of Literary and Typographic Anecdote*, a compilation from many sources of information about printers and stationers. Though few have the stamina to plow straight through its 996 pages, it contains a staggering amount of fascinating typographic information. The following anecdote about the celebrated typefounder Joseph Jackson's apprenticeship to William Caslon is a case in point:

> [He] had a great desire to learn the method of cutting the punches, which is, in general, kept profoundly secret. His master, and his master's father, constantly locked themselves in the place where they performed this part of the art; and in order to accomplish his object, Jackson bored a hole through the wainscot, and was thus, at different times, able to watch them through the process and to form some idea how the whole was performed: and he afterwards applied himself at every opportunity to the finishing of a punch. When he had completed one to his own mind he presented it to his master, expecting to be rewarded for his ingenuity; but the premium he received was a severe blow, with a threat that he should be sent to Bridewell if he again made a similar attempt.

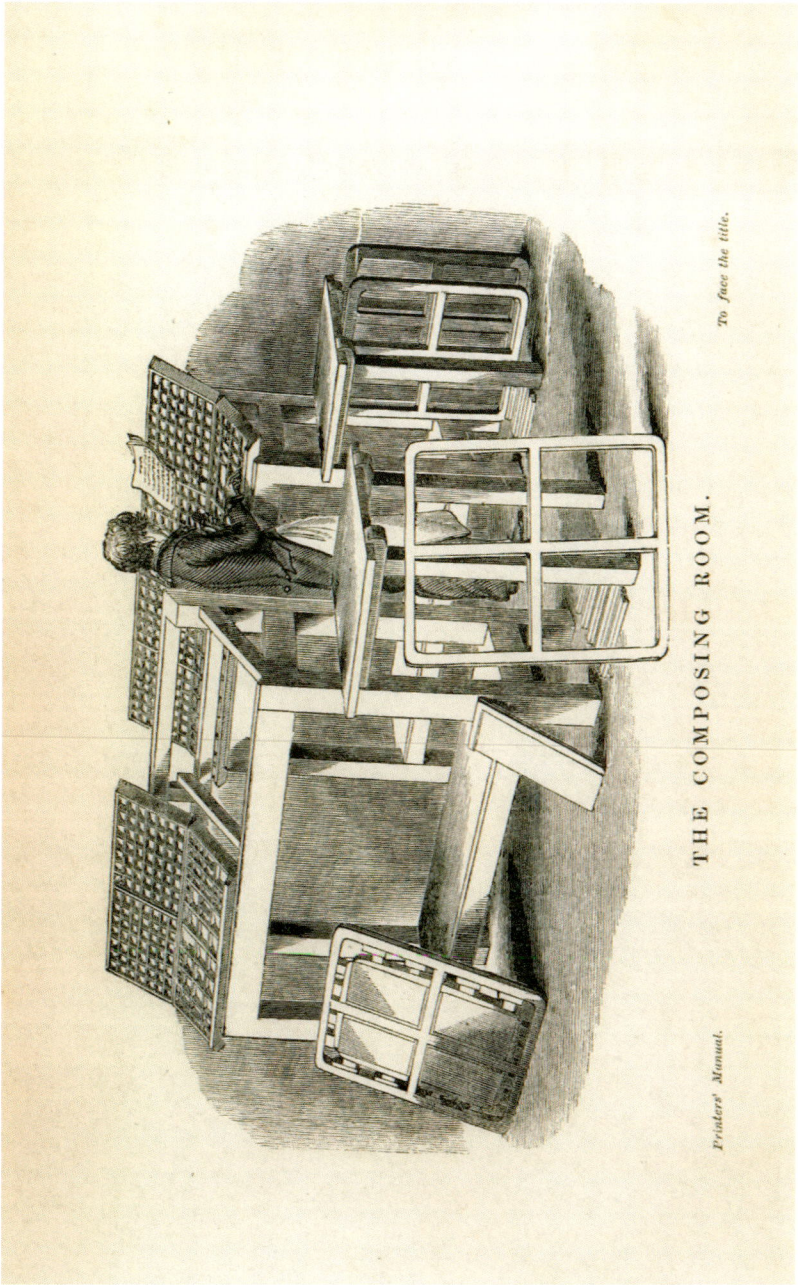

Printers' Manual.

THE COMPOSING ROOM.

To face the title.

39

William Savage

A Dictionary of the Art of Printing. London: Longman, Brown, Green and Longmans, 1841.

THE PUBLICATION OF SAVAGE's *Dictionary* marks a departure from earlier models of manuals on printing. The nature of the information remains the same—there are, for example, sections on composition, imposition, and presswork, but they are presented now in an alphabetical format along with hundreds of other entries describing various printing techniques or explaining terms used in the trade. Particular attention is given to fine presswork and the printing of wood-engravings.

Moxon is still regarded as an authority, but more often than not is used "to contrast the then method of printing with the present." Savage also faced the eternal problem of the encyclopedist: new discoveries and their applications to printing had to be incorporated even after the printing had begun. The process of electrotyping is one example. Despite the difficulties of age and the relentless march of progress, Savage toiled on. His book was written, he said, "with the hope that it might be placed in the hands of each printer's boy on entering the business …" This was a far cry from the attitude that had prevailed two centuries earlier.

No. 1. An Impression from an Engraving on Wood.

No. 2. An Impression from an Electrotype Copy of No. 1.

41

George Dodd

British Manufactures. Series VI. Books and Travelling.
London: Charles Knight, 1846.

THE AUTHOR'S PREFACE NOTES THAT "the details concerning print-ing and paper-making are mainly founded (with slight alterations) on four papers in the 'Penny Magazine' (Nos. 96, 101, 107, 112), written by a different hand from the rest of this volume." That hand, of course, was Charles Knight, who agreed to this republication of his essays in compact form. Even the wood-engravings were recut, with the larger ones being reduced in size.

The proportion in which a particular letter is required, renders it necessary that the cells of the lower case should be arranged not as the letters follow each other alphabetically, but that those in most frequent use should be nearest the hand of the compositor. The point to

The Compositor.

which he brings the letters, after picking them up out of their cells, is not far removed from the centre of the lower case; so that in a range of about six inches, on every side, he can obtain the e, d, e, i, s, m, n, h, o, p, u, t, a, and r, the letters in most frequent use. The spaces, which he waits for the division of every word,

lie close at his hand at the bottom of the central division of the lower case. It must be quite obvious that the man who contrived this arrangement saved a vast deal of time to the compositor. A stranger to the art is surprised at the accuracy with which a compositor dips his fingers into the box containing the letter which he requires. This surprise is generally connected with an opinion that the compositor would do his work more correctly if the boxes were labelled. A very inexpert performer upon the piano will, nevertheless, strike any one of the seventy-eight notes without making a mistake; and in the same way the youngest boy of a printing-office very soon learns the places of the letters without any difficulty.

Let us now for a little while follow the compositor in the progress of his work.

Standing before the pair of cases which contain the Roman letter, he holds in his left hand what is called a *composing-stick*. This is a little iron or brass frame, one side of which is moveable so that it may be adjusted to the required width of the page or column which the workman has to set up. It is made perfectly true and square; for without such accuracy the lines would be of unequal length. It is adapted to contain not more than about twelve lines of such type as the present.

Composing-Stick.

The copy from which the compositor works rests upon

The History of Printing. London: Printed for the Society for Promoting Christian Knowledge, 1855.

T HIS DELIGHTFUL WORK was published in two editions, 1855 and 1862. Though the title suggests that the book contains nothing more than a history, there is actually quite a bit of useful practical information including some splendid wood-engraved illustrations. There is a charming exuberance about the work and it is full of interesting, albeit moralizing anecdotes. The art of printing, for example, made it possible for the "poor and simple, as well as the rich and learned…to obey the command 'search the Scriptures.'"

The second edition contains expanded sections on printing for the blind, nature-printing, lithography, and calico printing. It is also graced with a handsome chromolithographic frontispiece.

Jacob Abbott

The Harper Establishment; or How the Story Books are Made. New York: Harper & Bros., 1855.

T HIS FASCINATING VOLUME was part of a series called the "Harper Story Books" which documented in "simple and lucid style" various subjects of appeal to children and adults alike. There is hardly a more valuable or detailed look into a mid-nineteenth century printing establishment and how books were made there than that revealed here, and this "story book" is, therefore, an indispensable resource for both printing and literary historians. In the introduction to a facsimile edition published in 1956, Jacob Blanck wrote that the Harper building, erected between 1853 and 1855, was "an architectural marvel: a printing plant designed for the ages and planned to forever withstand the attack of corrosion, dry rot, type lice, fire and other like perils."

In the same spirit of Charles Knight's *Penny Magazine*, Abbott painstakingly describes the construction of the building and gives a floor-by-floor account of the various bookmaking processes conducted on each. Thus, there are explanations of composition, proofing, punch- and matrix-making, typefounding, printing, wood-engraving, and binding. A liberal use of illustrations further enhances the book; particularly noteworthy is a fascinating cut-away side view of the entire building where minute figures bustle about their various and sundry tasks.

INTERIOR OF THE VAULTS.

Thomas Lynch

The Printer's Manual; A Practical Guide to Compositors and Pressmen. Cincinnati: Published by the Cincinnati Type-Foundry, 1866.

THE PREFACE OF LYNCH'S 1866 MANUAL indicates that the first edition of 1859 had gone out of print and that a new edition, reset in larger types, was called for. However, the author notes, "the state of the country being such that, as we know not what a day may bring forth, it is thought best to make the issue without other than minor alterations." Whether the publisher was lazy or the so-called "state of the country" truly discouraged the sale of printer's manuals would now be difficult to ascertain, but the same preface still graced the opening pages of the next edition, published six years later.

There appears to be no connection between this manual and those of Moxon and his followers. Instead, notes Sinclair Hitchings in his remarks on an exhibition of printer's manuals at Dartmouth College, Lynch "takes a direction largely independent of the old authors. Thomas Lynch and his publications deserve further investigation." The technical sections are excellent, especially those on imposition, presswork, and colored inks.

and lower-case are put, one above the other, at the same side of the case and in the order named. The dashes have been placed, according to size, in one row of boxes, and the commercial marks and $ are close to each other and directly in front of the compositor.

The following are the plans of the upper- and lower-cases :

UPPER CASE.

LOWER CASE.

CASING THE LETTER.

When the types are to be used continually, as on daily newspapers, there should be a pair of cases for every fifty pounds of types in the fount; because the capitals, figures,

R. Hoe & Company

Manufacturers of Type Revolving and Single and Double Cylinder Printing Machines...New-York: R. Hoe & Co., 1867.

As manufacturers of printing presses began selling increasingly complex machinery to the graphic arts industry during the nineteenth century, the need grew to provide detailed instructions on operation and maintenance. The Hoe Company, the largest such manufacturer in the country, acknowledged in this catalog the necessity for customer support. In addition to the usual descriptions of goods for sale, there are sections on setting up various printing machines and thorough directions for making ready on cylinder presses.

The high quality printing of the catalog suggests the hand of a master printer. Sure enough, on the back of the title page it is noted that the printing was accomplished by Francis Hart & Co. To those familiar with the career of the great printer Theodore Low De Vinne, the name of the Hart firm will strike a chord: it was there that De Vinne perfected his craft, became an expert on printing wood-engravings, and eventually rose to become a full partner, then owner of the company.

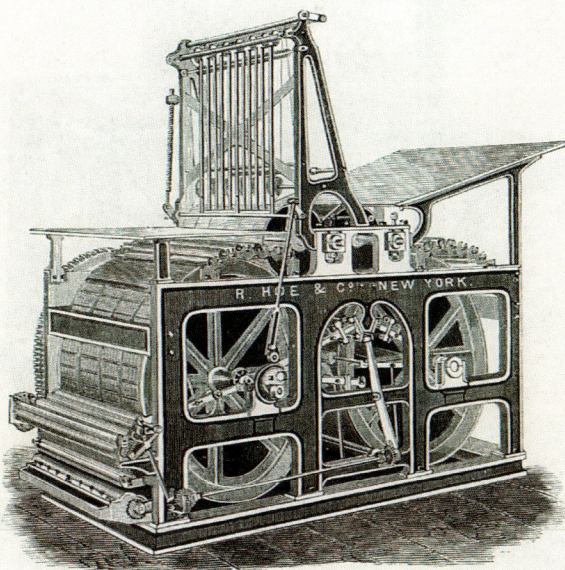

Type Revolving Book Perfecting Press.

As the name indicates, it is on the rotary principle, the forms being secured on the surface of two large horizontal cylinders. This system, as it does away with the reciprocating motion, admits of a greater speed in printing than any other. The distribution of the ink also is more perfect, there being room for six or more ink rollers to each form. It is equally well adapted to letter-press, stereotype and wood cut work, and will print from 1,500 to 2,000 perfected sheets per hour, the only limit to its speed being the capability of the feeder to supply the sheets.

As it dispenses with the registering apparatus, and is furnished with our patent self-acting sheet flyer, only one attendant is required for the largest sized press.

Thomas MacKellar

The American Printer: A Manual of Typography: Containing Complete Instructions for Beginners . . . Philadelphia: MacKellar, Smiths & Jordan, 1866–1893.

THE FIRST EDITION of this famous American printer's manual appeared in 1866 and was followed by seventeen more editions at various intervals for many years thereafter. The illustration shown here comes from the fifth edition of 1870. That edition also includes the Preface to the first edition which begins: "Usefulness rather than originality has been aimed at in the preparation of the American Printer ..." That said, MacKellar goes on to acknowledge his sources, the most important of which was Johnson's *Typographia*.

While the chapter headings for the most part remain the same, the later editions are longer, incorporating a good deal of updated material. The press section of the eleventh edition, for example, contains new information on job presses, just then beginning to revolutionize the short-run segment of the printing industry with their speed and convenience. There are also two additional chapters, one on how to set up a paying job-printing facility, the other on useful recipes for everything from directions on casting new rollers, to mucilage, to fire-proof ink! One interesting fact revealed in this chapter is that Russia-leather-covered books placed in a booksellers window "will destroy flies and other insects."

MacKellar was well-known for his sense of humor, vividly demonstrated in a section titled "Hints honored in the Breach." In Hint no. 3 he sarcastically advises the careless workman: "If a line is rather too tight to permit the last letter to get in easily, push it down hard with your rule or a quadrate. The type may be injured; but why didn't it fit in just right at first?"

HOE'S TYPE-REVOLVING MACHINE—FRONT VIEW.

19   SIDE VIEW.   217

Oscar H. Harpel

Harpel's Typograph, or Book of Specimens Containing Useful Information, Suggestions and a Collection of Examples of Letterpress Job Printing ... Cincinnati: Printed and Published by the Author, 1870.

THE TYPOGRAPH IS ONE OF THE MOST INTRIGUING printer's manuals of the nineteenth century and one of the most delightful to browse. Ostensibly produced to answer the need for a "more practical hand-book and guide, than any at present available, for the use of novices and unskilled workmen,..." the work is mostly a showcase of samples of job printing executed at Harpel's Cincinnati firm.

Instructions for setting up a profitable office, hints on the most appropriate types and equipment to buy, and chapters on composition, imposition, and recommendations on inks and rollers take up the first 48 pages. The next 175 pages or so contain job printing specimens "taken from the current transactions of a regular printing office, and were not especially designed for the pages of the book." Many of these are in color, and Harpel tells us in a closing note at the back that 476,000 impressions were required to print less than 3,000 copies of the book. Among several fold-out plates is an elaborate mortgage bond for the Route "9" Street Railway Company of Cincinnati. Harpel was among the first to recognize the potential of platen presses and he showed that job printing could be a profitable niche for the aspiring printer.

Cincinnati Type Foundry.

PRINTING TYPE PRESS MATERIAL

No. 201 Vine Street, Cincinnati.

C. WELLS,
Treas.

K. BARTH.
W. F. HUNT.

BOURBON

WHISKEY

Brachmann & Massard,

No. 81 WEST THIRD STREET, near Vine,

CINCINNATI. OHIO.

Harpel, Pr. Cin.

55

Joseph Gould

The Letter-Press Printer: A Complete Guide to the Art of Printing. London: Farrington & Co., 1876.

THIS NO-NONSENSE MANUAL was designed to be an economical, workmanlike guide to the trade of printing. Its various diagrams of imposition, tables of wages and abbreviations, and lists of definitions make it a useful, if not especially handsome manual. The first edition of 3,000 copies was published in 1876 and was described by the historian Geoffrey Wakeman as the "first good comprehensive manual to appear in [the latter] half of the century." The author later claimed to be "astonished by the fact that the whole 3000 copies were sold in less than three years."

The publication of the second edition in 1881 was attended by disaster—the stereotype plates were flawed, the printing was hurried, and one of Gould's sons died suddenly of a broken blood vessel in his lungs during the printing of the book.

The following is the common " lay " of the Lower Case, and is almost universally used, with a few slight alterations, although it is capable of being greatly improved. But those who have the courage to make many alterations and improvements in the " lay " of the lower case are usually rewarded by having their cases extensively " pied " by strangers who are occasionally called in to assist, and who, not being used to the altered lay, take some time to become sufficiently acquainted with it to be able to distribute into cases different from those they have been used to, so that the common lay is usually interfered with as little as possible. A very great improvement, however, with little alteration of the cases, might be introduced by having the thin and middle spaces close to the thick, the distance between them as they stand causing extra labour and a great loss of time in spacing. In double-cases the same " lay " is adopted, but the small-cap portion of the upper case is omitted.

c 2

fl	ff	fi	Em-quadrats.	Quadrats.
(	⊥	)	En-quadrats.	
..	g	w	..	.
?	f	,	q	.
!	s	p		r
— (Thin a'd Middle space)		y		
	i	o		a
	e	h	Thick Space.	
j	d	n		t
œ	c	m		n
æ	b	l		v
—	&	ffl	ffi (Hair Space)	z	x

Composing Room Lectures: A Manual for Young Printers. By an Old Printer. 3d. ed. London: Published at the Press News Office, 1881.

Printing Office Characters: or, "Types" of Printing-Office Life, by an Old Printer. London: Press News Office, 1881.

T HESE SLIM TRACTS ARE THE WORK of the so-called "Old Printer." The *Lectures* exhibit an unyielding Victorian moral tone that grinds away at the reader like a dull file. Consider the inspiring first sentence: "Printing may not be the most lucrative profession for a young man to get his living at, but still, it is very far from being the worst." Later, the young printer is cautioned against becoming too enamoured of the life of a newspaper reporter. The Old Printer notes severely that, "'Literary drudge and publishing-office fag' would be the better name for such a position than that of Reporter."

Characters, on the other hand, while carrying its own moral baggage, is not quite so heavy-handed, and makes an attempt at amusing the reader by creating such caricatures of typical printing-office "types" as "Mr. Fussy, the Windbag," "Mr. Phil Rushasbout," and "The Turn-over," the ne'er-do-well journeyman printer who can never hold down a steady job.

PRINTING-OFFICE CHARACTERS;

OR,

"Types" of Printing-office Life.

BY

AN OLD PRINTER.

[REPRINTED FROM "PRESS NEWS."]

LONDON:
PUBLISHED BY DORRINGTON BROS., WINDSOR COURT, STRAND.
1881.

PRICE TWOPENCE.

59

Samuel Whybrew

The Progressive Printer; A Book of Instruction for Journeymen and Apprenticed Printers. 2d. ed. Rochester, N.Y., Whybrew & Ripley, 1882.

THIS LITTLE BOOK PROPOSES to stimulate the ambitions of those who are "desirous of becoming masters of the art typographical." It, therefore, does not pretend to be an exhaustive treatise, but instead suggests appropriate sources for detailed information, chiefly the manual of MacKellar and various periodicals devoted to printing. Even so, there are many general instructions, hints, and cautions, including a diatribe against "amateur" printers: "one might as well hope to pump water from an empty well as to expect originality and skill from a sham printer."

Oddly, for a book intended to stimulate ambition in the trade, it begins with a Poe-esque poem—"The Old Printer"—so lugubrious and mournful that any young printer in his right mind who read it would immediately contemplate a career change. Here is the first verse:

> A printer stood at his case one night,
>> in his office dark and drear,
> And his weary sight was as dim as the light
>> of the moldy lamp hung near;
> The wintry winds were howling without,
>> and the snow falling thick and fast,
> But the printer, I trow, shook his locks of snow,
>> and laughed at the shrieking blast;
> He watched the hands of the clock creep round,
>> keeping time with his snail-like tick,
> As he gathered the type, with a weary click,
>> in his old rust-eaten stick.

H. G. Bishop

The Practical Printer; A Book of Instruction for Beginners: A Book of Reference for the More Advanced. Albany: H. G. Bishop, 1889.

BISHOP ENJOYED A DUAL CAREER. Not only was he a practicing printer, he was also a prolific writer about the profession. During the 1880s he was a contributor to *The Inland Printer*, just then beginning to achieve fame as one of the most respected and well-produced printing trade journals in the country. Bishop was characteristic of a new breed of printers who urged a theoretical study of the printing business in addition to a thorough grounding in the practical aspects of the craft. "It is of the utmost importance that a man should have a practical knowledge of his business," he wrote, "but unless he knows the theory, as well as the practice, he has no *knowledge* of it at all." Thus the "how-to" sections, imposition diagrams, and tables normally found in most manuals are bolstered in Bishop's work by a chapter on "Business Management."

REDUCED FACSIMILE OF THE HANDWRITING OF AN EDITOR, WHICH SHOWS HIS
GENERAL STYLE OF WRITING FOR THE PRESS.

And this is by no means the worst he can get, as many a compositor knows to his sorrow. And yet there are compositors who can read such scrawls, who know how to wind themselves into the intricacies of the worst writing; and the way they do it is by closely examining the author's style (for most authors have a style, however bad

John F. Earhart

The Color Printer; A Treatise on the Use of Colors in Typographic Printing. Cincinnati, Ohio: Earhart & Richardson, 1892.

JOHN EARHART WORKED ON THIS LANDMARK of American color printing for more than four years, making up 625 type formes and printing 1,625,000 impressions for the small number of copies that comprised the edition. Most of the illustrations were intended to show color harmonies and how tints in various strengths could be combined. Incredibly, he was able to produce more than 1,000 distinct color and tint values from just twelve stock inks. Earhart also provides examples of embossing, rainbow fountain printing, and special tonal effects.

The book was enormously influential, and prompted George Joiner, author of *Fine Printing* (1895), to write that Earhart's "genius as author and manipulator of the "Color Printer" gives him a foremost position amongst the galaxy of American artist-printers…" Earhart accomplished most of his work on a Colt's Armory platen press, a machine capable of printing multi-color images in tight register.

PLATE 65

═ COLT'S ARMORY ═
PRINTING AND EMBOSSING PRESSES

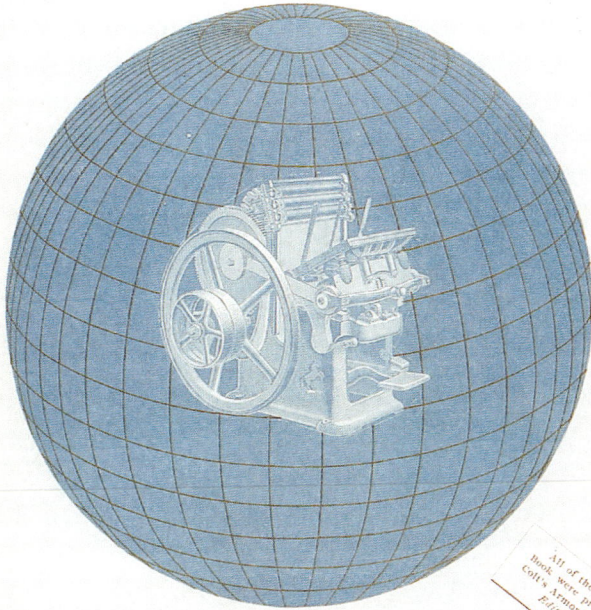

All of the Plates in this Book were printed on the Colt's Armory Presses. *Editor Color Printer.*

THE BEST ON EARTH.

SEND FOR COMPLETE ILLUSTRATED CATALOGUE

JOHN THOMSON PRESS COMPANY,
··· 212 TEMPLE COURT, NEW YORK ···

349
67, Gold and 36

65

George Joiner

Fine Printing: Its Inception, Development, and Practice. London: Printed and published by Cooper and Budd, 1895.

THIS TEXT IS A DIRECT OUTCOME of the Artistic Printing movement that enjoyed great popularity during the late nineteenth century. Responding to the increasing competition from lithography, letterpress printers (and type foundries) sought to demonstrate that relief printing on highly finished coated paper was capable of producing amazingly detailed and exquisitely colored work that rose to the level of fine art—a goal embraced just as keenly by the chromolithographers of the time. The author of this work credits Oscar Harpel and his *Typograph* (1870) with "making more good printers than any other typographic handbook produced up to that time." A little healthy competition didn't hurt either, and printers were inspired to ever greater feats of typographical complexity through the agency of the "Printers' International Specimen Exchange."

Joiner's instructions are clear and precise, and there is an emphasis on careful preparation and good workmanship, from controlling composition costs all the way through to cleaning the press rollers. The illustrations are especially interesting and include examples of typical German, American, and British typographic styles.

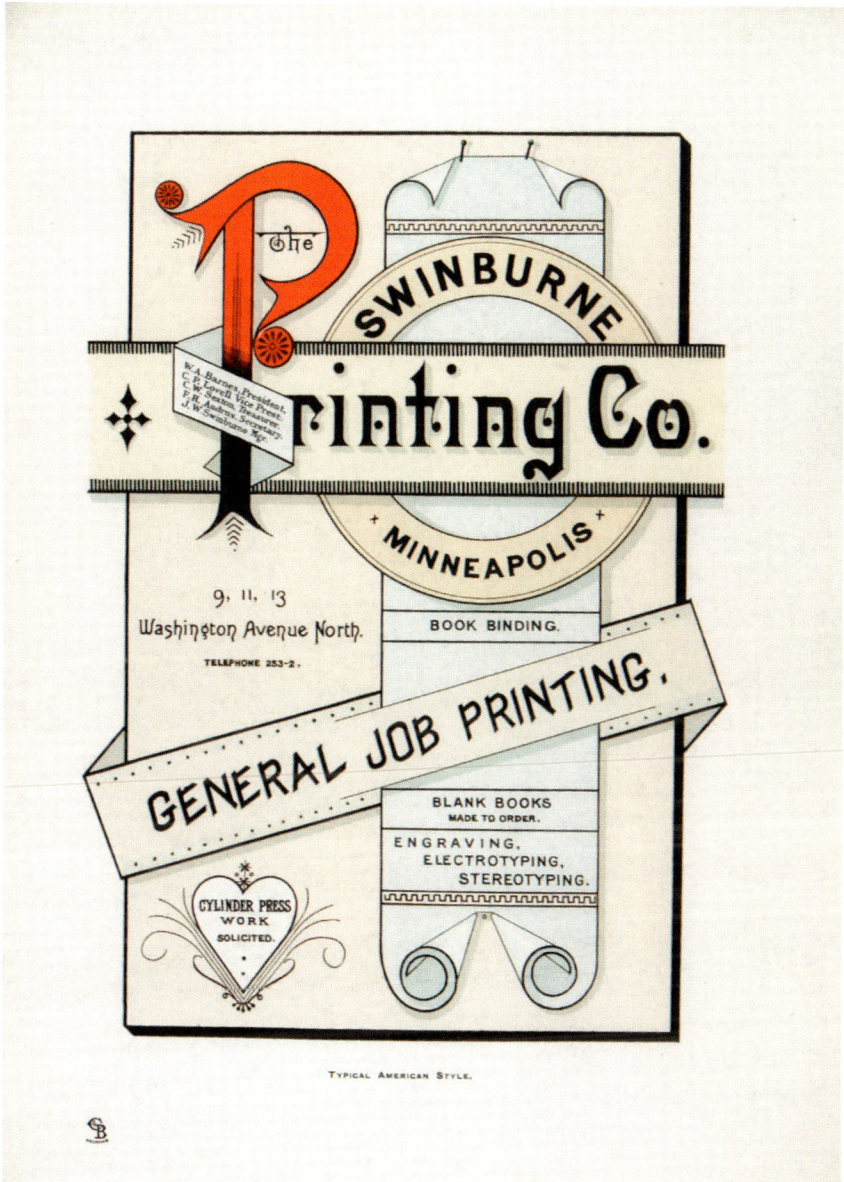

The Swinburne Printing Co.

SWINBURNE
Printing Co.
MINNEAPOLIS

W. A. Barnes, President.
C. M. Lovell, Vice Prest.
C. H. Sabin, Treasurer.
F. H. Sabin, Secretary.
J. W. Swinburne, Mgr.

9, 11, 13
Washington Avenue North.
TELEPHONE 253-2.

BOOK BINDING.

GENERAL JOB PRINTING.

BLANK BOOKS
MADE TO ORDER.

ENGRAVING,
ELECTROTYPING,
STEREOTYPING.

CYLINDER PRESS
WORK
SOLICITED.

TYPICAL AMERICAN STYLE.

67

Theodore Low De Vinne

Plain Printing Types. New York: Oswald Publishing Co., 1900.

Correct Composition. New York: Oswald Publishing Co., 1901.

A Treatise on Title-Pages. New York: Oswald Publishing Co., 1902.

Modern Methods of Book Composition. New York: Oswald Publishing Co., 1904.

Beginning in 1900, under the general series title *The Practice of Typography*, Theodore Low De Vinne issued one of the most comprehensive sets of manuals on type—its design, manufacture, and composition—ever made available to the public. Up to then, the standard all-purpose manual had been Thomas MacKellar's *American Printer*—all eighteen editions of it. Perhaps De Vinne recognized the tendency in many printers to concentrate their attention on the pressroom at the expense of the composing room. At any rate, the only area not covered in this marvelous series is presswork; certainly, from this point on, most manuals tended to be specialized.

De Vinne was one of the most respected figures in American printing during this period and wrote voluminously on all aspects of his profession. Bigmore and Wyman remark that "besides being a constant contributor to most of the trade journals, he has written a number articles in various periodicals on printing and its history; and for several years has taken an active and influential part in trade politics at New York, where he carries on an extensive printing business."

As an ardent historian of printing, founding member of the Grolier Club in New York, and an individual who tirelessly promoted the ideals of his profession, there was no one more qualified to write a treatise on typography. The text was entirely original and reflected De Vinne's extensive knowledge and experience as a practicing printer. His books remain, to this day, essential reading for anyone interested in pursuing a career as a typographer, if not also as a printer.

View of body inclined
to show the face.

Letter H, from a type
of canon body.

Face of the letter
on the body.

1 counter.
2 hair-line.
3 serif.
4 stem, or body-mark.
5 neck, or beard.

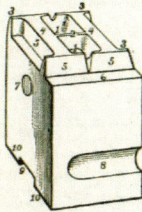

6 shoulder.
7 pin mark.
8 nick.
9 groove.
10 feet.

Spaces of Pica

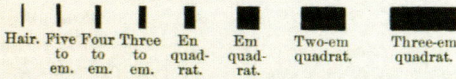

Hair. | Five to em. | Four to em. | Three to em. | En quad-rat. | Em quad-rat. | Two-em quadrat. | Three-em quadrat.

Dimensions of Bodies

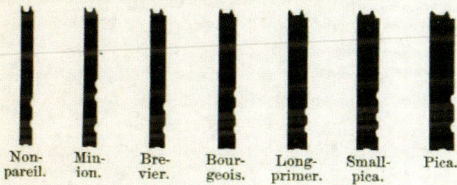

Non-pareil. | Min-ion. | Bre-vier. | Bour-geois. | Long-primer. | Small-pica. | Pica.

COLOPHON

*Text based on an exhibition in the Cary Graphic Arts Collection
and later reformatted as a graduate student publishing project
by Barbara Day, 2002*

*Design and Production, 2005
Marnie Soom*

*Photography
Christina Almeida*

*Printing
Lulu.com*